WILLIAM MORRIS: Arts and Crafts Designs

A Book of Postcards

SAN FRANCISCO

Pomegranate Communications, Inc.
19018 NE Portal Way, Portland OR 97230
800 227 1428; www.pomegranate.com

Pomegranate Europe Ltd.
Unit 1, Heathcote Business Centre, Hurlbutt Road
Warwick, Warwickshire CV34 6TD, UK
[+44] 0 1926 430111; sales@pomeurope.co.uk

ISBN 978-0-7649-3283-0
Pomegranate Catalog No. AA300

Pomegranate publishes books of postcards on a wide range of subjects.
Please contact the publisher for more information.

Cover designed by Lora Santiago
Printed in China
22 21 20 19 18 17 16 15 14 13   13 12 11 10 9 8 7 6 5 4

To facilitate detachment of the postcards from this book, fold each card along its perforation line before tearing.

William Morris was a lifelong opponent of mass production. Through his writings and his design work, Morris offered, in rebuttal to the shabby products of mechanized industry, a vision of the integrity of craft and craftsman. He believed that art should be a part of every person's life and disdained the accumulation of expensive but useless (and aesthetically valueless) artifacts by a well-heeled but undiscerning elite.

Believing that art could and should find expression in utilitarian objects that could be enjoyed as part of everyday life, Morris (English, 1834–1896) worked in a wide range of fields, including textiles, furniture, tiles, glass, and wallpaper. By the 1890s he was a legend not only in England but throughout the world. His sensibility dramatically influenced typography, printing, and interior design.

Morris created his first wallpaper in 1864; over the following thirty-two years he completed forty-nine wallpaper designs and five ceiling designs, almost all employing floral, fruit, or foliage motifs. He was concerned that his designs be straightforwardly two-dimensional (if highly complex within those two dimensions), in keeping with the two-dimensional nature of wallpaper itself. In other words, Morris never imitated other materials or created the illusion of three dimensions.

The thirty designs reproduced in this book of postcards are reproduced from two Morris and Co. wallpaper sample books in the collection of the Brooklyn Museum.

WILLIAM MORRIS: Arts and Crafts Designs

Arcadia pattern

William Morris and Co., Ltd.
London, England, before 1917
Wallpaper sample book
Brooklyn Museum (71.151.2-141)
Purchased with funds given by Mrs. and Mrs. Carl Selden and
Designated Purchase Fund
© Brooklyn Museum

WILLIAM MORRIS: Arts and Crafts Designs

Artichoke pattern

BOX 808022 PETALUMA CA 94975

Pomegranate

William Morris and Co., Ltd.
London, England, before 1917
Wallpaper sample book
Brooklyn Museum (71.151.1-110)
Purchased with funds given by Mrs. and Mrs. Carl Selden and
Designated Purchase Fund

WILLIAM MORRIS: Arts and Crafts Designs

Norwich pattern

BOX 808022   PETALUMA   CA 94975

Pomegranate

William Morris and Co., Ltd.
London, England, before 1917
Wallpaper sample book
Brooklyn Museum (71.151.1-104)
Purchased with funds given by Mrs. and Mrs. Carl Selden and
Designated Purchase Fund

WILLIAM MORRIS: Arts and Crafts Designs

Leicester pattern

BOX 808022   PETALUMA   CA 94975

Pomegranate

William Morris and Co., Ltd.
London, England, before 1917
Wallpaper sample book
Brooklyn Museum (71.151.1-33)
Purchased with funds given by Mrs. and Mrs. Carl Selden and
Designated Purchase Fund
© Brooklyn Museum

WILLIAM MORRIS: Arts and Crafts Designs

Autumn Flower pattern

CA 94975

PETALUMA

BOX 808022

Pomegranate

William Morris and Co., Ltd.
London, England, before 1917
Wallpaper sample book
Brooklyn Museum (71.151.1-108)
Purchased with funds given by Mrs. and Mrs. Carl Selden and
Designated Purchase Fund

WILLIAM MORRIS: Arts and Crafts Designs

Harebell pattern

BOX 808022   PETALUMA   CA 94975

Pomegranate

WILLIAM MORRIS: Arts and Crafts Designs

Bird and Anemone pattern

BOX 808022   PETALUMA   CA 94975

Pomegranate

WILLIAM MORRIS: Arts and Crafts Designs

Bower pattern

CA 94975

PETALUMA

BOX 808022

Pomegranate

William Morris and Co., Ltd.
London, England, before 1917
Wallpaper sample book
Brooklyn Museum (71.151.1-47)
Purchased with funds given by Mrs. and Mrs. Carl Selden and
Designated Purchase Fund

WILLIAM MORRIS: Arts and Crafts Designs
Fruit pattern

CA 94975 PETALUMA BOX 808022

Pomegranate

William Morris and Co., Ltd.
London, England, before 1917
Wallpaper sample book
Brooklyn Museum (71.151.1-64)
Purchased with funds given by Mrs. and Mrs. Carl Selden and
Designated Purchase Fund
© Brooklyn Museum

WILLIAM MORRIS: Arts and Crafts Designs

Daisy pattern

BOX 808022   PETALUMA   CA 94975

Pomegranate

William Morris and Co., Ltd.
London, England, before 1917
Wallpaper sample book
Brooklyn Museum (71.151.1-38)
Purchased with funds given by Mrs. and Mrs. Carl Selden and
Designated Purchase Fund

WILLIAM MORRIS: Arts and Crafts Designs

Pink and Rose pattern

BOX 808022   PETALUMA   CA 94975

Pomegranate

William Morris and Co., Ltd.
London, England, before 1917
Wallpaper sample book
Brooklyn Museum (71.151.2-111)
Purchased with funds given by Mrs. and Mrs. Carl Selden and
Designated Purchase Fund

WILLIAM MORRIS: Arts and Crafts Designs

Persian pattern

BOX 808022   PETALUMA   CA 94975

Pomegranate

William Morris and Co., Ltd.
London, England, before 1917
Wallpaper sample book
Brooklyn Museum (71.151.1-25)
Purchased with funds given by Mrs. and Mrs. Carl Selden and
Designated Purchase Fund

WILLIAM MORRIS: Arts and Crafts Designs

Willow Bough pattern

BOX 808022 PETALUMA CA 94975

Pomegranate

William Morris and Co., Ltd.
London, England, before 1917
Wallpaper sample book
Brooklyn Museum (71.151.1-18)
Purchased with funds given by Mrs. and Mrs. Carl Selden and
Designated Purchase Fund
© Brooklyn Museum

WILLIAM MORRIS: Arts and Crafts Designs

Brocade pattern

CA 94975

PETALUMA

BOX 808022

Pomegranate

William Morris and Co., Ltd.
London, England, before 1917
Wallpaper sample book
Brooklyn Museum (71.151.1-31)
Purchased with funds given by Mrs. and Mrs. Carl Selden and
Designated Purchase Fund
© Brooklyn Museum

WILLIAM MORRIS: Arts and Crafts Designs

Blossom pattern

CA 94975

PETALUMA

BOX 808022

Pomegranate

William Morris and Co., Ltd.
London, England, before 1917
Wallpaper sample book
Brooklyn Museum (71.151.1-18)
Purchased with funds given by Mrs. and Mrs. Carl Selden and
Designated Purchase Fund

WILLIAM MORRIS: Arts and Crafts Designs

Myrtle pattern

CA 94975

PETALUMA

BOX 808022

Pomegranate

William Morris and Co., Ltd.
London, England, before 1917
Wallpaper sample book
Brooklyn Museum (71.151.1-77)
Purchased with funds given by Mrs. and Mrs. Carl Selden and
Designated Purchase Fund

WILLIAM MORRIS: Arts and Crafts Designs

Garden pattern

CA 94975

PETALUMA

BOX 808022

Pomegranate

William Morris and Co., Ltd.
London, England, before 1917
Wallpaper sample book
Brooklyn Museum (71.151.1-76)
Purchased with funds given by Mrs. and Mrs. Carl Selden and
Designated Purchase Fund

WILLIAM MORRIS: Arts and Crafts Designs
Arbutus pattern

CA 94975

PETALUMA

BOX 808022

Pomegranate

William Morris and Co., Ltd.
London, England, before 1917
Wallpaper sample book
Brooklyn Museum (71.151.1-63)
Purchased with funds given by Mrs. and Mrs. Carl Selden and
Designated Purchase Fund

WILLIAM MORRIS: Arts and Crafts Designs

Larkspur pattern

CA 94975

PETALUMA

BOX 808022

Pomegranate

William Morris and Co., Ltd.
London, England, before 1917
Wallpaper sample book
Brooklyn Museum (71.151.1-41)
Purchased with funds given by Mrs. and Mrs. Carl Selden and
Designated Purchase Fund

WILLIAM MORRIS: Arts and Crafts Designs

Seaweed pattern

BOX 808022   PETALUMA   CA 94975

Pomegranate

William Morris and Co., Ltd.
London, England, before 1917
Wallpaper sample book
Brooklyn Museum (71.151.1-86)
Purchased with funds given by Mrs. and Mrs. Carl Selden and
Designated Purchase Fund

WILLIAM MORRIS: Arts and Crafts Designs

Orchard pattern

CA 94975

PETALUMA

BOX 808022

Pomegranate

William Morris and Co., Ltd.
London, England, before 1917
Wallpaper sample book
Brooklyn Museum (71.151.1-85)
Purchased with funds given by Mrs. and Mrs. Carl Selden and
Designated Purchase Fund

WILLIAM MORRIS: Arts and Crafts Designs

Sweet Pea pattern

CA 94975

PETALUMA

BOX 808022

Pomegranate

William Morris and Co., Ltd.
London, England, before 1917
Wallpaper sample book
Brooklyn Museum (71.151.1-35)
Purchased with funds given by Mrs. and Mrs. Carl Selden and
Designated Purchase Fund

WILLIAM MORRIS: Arts and Crafts Designs

Indian pattern

BOX 808022   PETALUMA   CA 94975

Pomegranate

William Morris and Co., Ltd.
London, England, before 1917
Wallpaper sample book
Brooklyn Museum (71.151.2-31)
Purchased with funds given by Mrs. and Mrs. Carl Selden and
Designated Purchase Fund

WILLIAM MORRIS: Arts and Crafts Designs

Blackthorn pattern

CA 94975

PETALUMA

BOX 808022

Pomegranate

William Morris and Co., Ltd.
London, England, before 1917
Wallpaper sample book
Brooklyn Museum (71.151.1-125)
Purchased with funds given by Mrs. and Mrs. Carl Selden and
Designated Purchase Fund
© Brooklyn Museum

WILLIAM MORRIS: Arts and Crafts Designs

Hyacinth pattern

CA 94975

PETALUMA

BOX 808022

Pomegranate

William Morris and Co., Ltd.
London, England, before 1917
Wallpaper sample book
Brooklyn Museum (71.151.1-29)
Purchased with funds given by Mrs. and Mrs. Carl Selden and
Designated Purchase Fund
© Brooklyn Museum

WILLIAM MORRIS: Arts and Crafts Designs

Grapevine pattern

CA 94975

PETALUMA

BOX 808022

Pomegranate

William Morris and Co., Ltd.
London, England, before 1917
Wallpaper sample book
Brooklyn Museum (71.151.1-109)
Purchased with funds given by Mrs. and Mrs. Carl Selden and
Designated Purchase Fund

WILLIAM MORRIS: Arts and Crafts Designs

Chrysanthemum pattern

CA 94975

PETALUMA

BOX 808022

Pomegranate

William Morris and Co., Ltd.
London, England, before 1917
Wallpaper sample book
Brooklyn Museum (71.151.1-93)
Purchased with funds given by Mrs. and Mrs. Carl Selden and
Designated Purchase Fund

CA 94975

PETALUMA

BOX 808022

Pomegranate

William Morris and Co., Ltd.
London, England, before 1917
Wallpaper sample book
Brooklyn Museum (71.151.1-49)
Purchased with funds given by Mrs. and Mrs. Carl Selden and
Designated Purchase Fund